SO, MRS. SMITH, YOU SAY YOU'RE 35 AND YOU STILL LIKE TO PLAY WITH BLOCKS!

A BOOK OF QUILTING BLOCKS AND HUMOR

BY
JOHN SHIMP

PUBLISHING

112 -31st Street, P. O. Box 6753
Wheeling, WV 26003

This book is dedicated, as am I, to Mimi.

ACKNOWLEDGMENTS

All of the characters in this book are fictitious, and any resemblance to actual persons, living or dead, is purely coincidental.

All quilts designed by the author. Unless otherwise stated, the quilts in this book were pieced and quilted by John Shimp or Mimi Shimp. Special thanks goes to the following individuals for their help in making some of the quilts:

Tula Bailey, Tula's Treasures, 3765 Grass Valley Hwy. #227, Auburn, CA.
Kaye England, Quilt Quarters, 600 Main Street, Carmel, IN.
Jean Humenansky, The Country Peddler, 2242 Carter Ave., St. Paul, MN.
Jan Krueger, Hearthside Quilters' Nook, 10731 W. Forest Home, Hales Corners, WI.
Jenny McDermid, Freckles', 112 -10 Street, Calgary, Alberta, Canada.
Edith Mitchell, Tupper Lake, NY.
Barbara Spielberg, Los Angeles, CA.

and for their machine quilting expertise:

Leta Brazell, The Quiltworks, 11117 Menaul NE, Albuquerque, NM.
        Sawtooth, Egyptian Fantasy, The Wedding Quilt.
Susan Godkin, Oakdale Stitching Post, 126 N. Yosemite, Oakdale, CA.
        Amish Ribbons, JuJuBees, BBQ.
Jan Krueger, Hearthside Quilters' Nook, 10731 W. Forest Home, Hales Corners, WI.
        Irish Chain Illusion.

And a very special thanks to Dawn Hall, Cherrywood Fabrics, Baxter, MN, for the hand dyed fabrics provided for Red Licorice.

ISBN 1-879844-04-4

Color scanning and separation of photographs by Color Chromatics, Torrance, CA.
Graphic design and layout by SPPS, 9753 Hampton Court, Fountain Valley, C 927098.
Linotronic film services by Imagination Graphics, Santa Ana, CA.
Photography by John Limboker, Huntington Beach, CA.
Printed in the USA by Boyd Press, Wheeling, WV.

Table of Contents

IT STARTS OUT SO SIMPLE

One of the things you normally do in quilting is to set up your design in a repeat (otherwise you have a meandering quilt design – not to say that this is bad, but it makes for difficulty in piecing if all the blocks are different.) There are circumstances where this is not desirable. But those times are really up to the quilter. This book contains designs that for the most part are based on repeats of one block, two blocks, or combinations of blocks in different orientations. There are really two basic repeats that I dwell on. These are based on 90° symmetry (the block looks the same when rotated 90°) and 180° symmetry (the block looks the same when rotated 180°.) Needless to say, 90° symmetry is also 180° symmetry but the reverse is not true.

Here I give an example of developing 90° symmetry. I am trying to develop an eight patch. To do this, I really break it down to a four patch.

This is a relatively random placement of some triangles, squares, and rectangles.

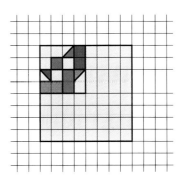

Repeat the design in a second four patch, and rotate it 90° (in either direction.)

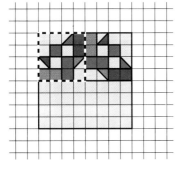

Add two more four patches, rotated 180° and 270° (in the same direction as the first.)

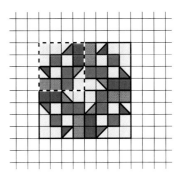

Now you have an eight patch block that you can rotate any which way and it still looks the same.

Of course, you may wish to do some playing with the placement of your pieces in the four patch to gain the desired effect where the corners come together (not only in the center of the resulting eight patch, but the corners where the eight patches come together.)

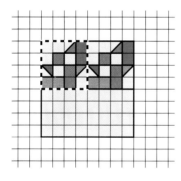

Let's take the first quarter of the eight patch and duplicate it side-by-side to form the top (or bottom) of another eight patch.

Repeat and rotate the four patches 180° and place them underneath the first two.

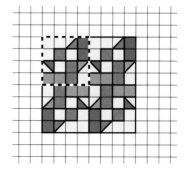

Now you have an eight patch block that you can rotate 180° and it still looks the same, but is different when you rotate it 90°. Therefore, you can do the same with this eight patch as you did with the four patch earlier to get a 90° symmetric sixteen patch.

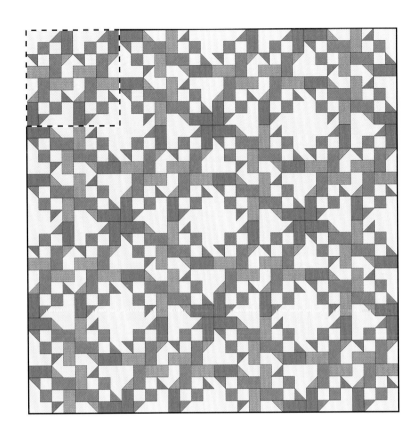

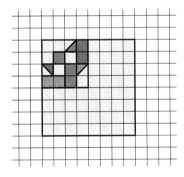

This time we'll start with the same four patch,

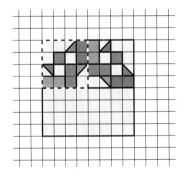

repeat it and rotate it 90°,

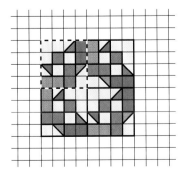

and alternate these two to get this eight patch. The eight patch is the repeat of the set of four shown to the right.

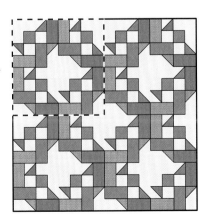

Just for kicks (that's what it's all about, isn't it?) let's do the 90° symmetry trick with this eight patch. Now a new pattern develops.

The point of all this is that there are many ways to put a simple four, eight, or other patch together. Which ones look best will be determined by the structure of the basic block.

From here on, you will see me use these (and other similar) simple techniques on the block designs in this book.

Dr. Ribbonkopf became confused while trying to understand Mrs. Smith's ecstacy with playing with the pieced block. When she finished explaining, his head, not unlike Mrs. Smith's blocks, was spinning. Luckily his head was screwed on more than one twist that day.

Quilting Primer: The Stash

See Mary go to the closet to get her fabric out. Mary will make a quilt.

See Mary get a chair to reach the top fabric in her stash. Can you say "stash"? She is stretching to reach the fabric.

Stretch, Mary, stretch. Oops.

Mary made the stack of fabric fall to the floor. See the mess it is in? Mess! Mess! Mess! Pick it up, Mary, for crying out loud. Can you say mess? Can you make a mess? Of course you can!

Look how neat it is after Mary has picked it up and folded it again. Now Mary is pooped. Pooped! Pooped! Pooped! Can you spell pooped? After all this folding, Mary is about to fold. Look, Mary! Look! You put the fabric you wanted on the bottom of the pile. Uh oh! Mary is making another mess. I guess Mary will try to sew another day. After she finishes folding.

Lessons To Learn

1. Mary, like all quilters, keeps a "stash" of fabric around for making quilts so she doesn't have to run down to her local quilt shop for every project. Actually, she still runs down to the local quilt shop anyway. You see, she is as into the care and feeding of her stash as she is into making quilts. How do you think her closet got into that predicament? Can you say predicament?

2. This brings us to the next lesson: find a good place to put your stash of fabric. If you don't have the closet space, add a room onto the house. Better yet, get a bigger house. If you want to, and can be satisfied with fantasy, just spend a lot of time at your local quilt shop and greet people at the door and tell them this is "my stash".

Positive - Negative

I will only discuss a couple of ways that I use to design a positive-negative quilt. One important piece of information to note is that, except for any borders you may apply, the quilt will consist of only two fabrics; and when you design it using these techniques, the same amount of each fabric is needed. Normally, the two fabrics may be chosen to be negatives of each other. For example, a black and a white, or a blue and a yellow. They don't necessarily have to be color opposites, but they should be very high contrast.

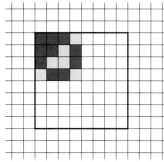

Again, we start with a simple four patch with two contrasting fabrics and put in a design of our choosing (no symmetry considered at this point.)

Now, repeat the four patch, completely opposite of the first one (light where dark was and vice versa.)

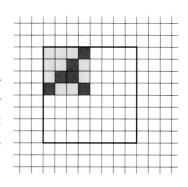

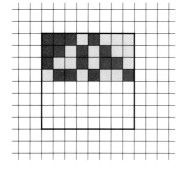

Now, place the second four patch next to the first one. I have rotated it 90° here. This gives a block that is its own negative when rotated 90°.

Finally, add two more blocks. This is done by duplicating the first two and rotating the pair 180° and placing them underneath the first pair.

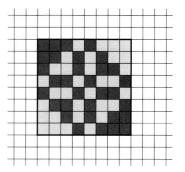

Block
Construction

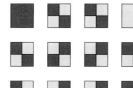

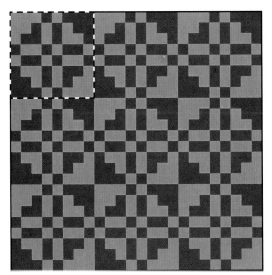

The block gives an interesting look in both diagonal directions.

Even though the block is positive-negative, the choice of fabrics can give one or the other the predominant effect in the design. It also depends on the observer as to which dominates.

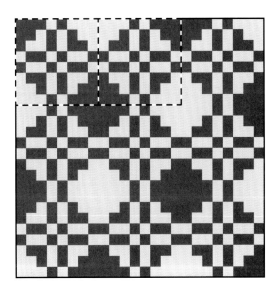

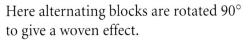

Here alternating blocks are rotated 90° to give a woven effect.

In fact, let's change the alternate blocks to a different pair of colors.

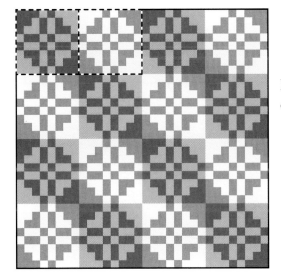

Hearts Delight
42" x 62"

Irish Chain Illusion
72" x 92"
quilted by Jan Krueger

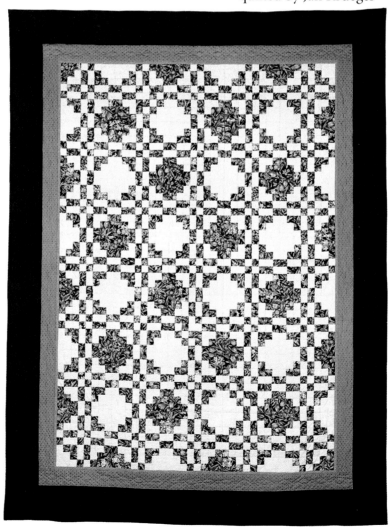

HEARTS IN POSITIVE AND NEGATIVE

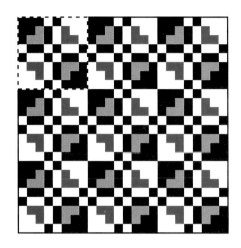

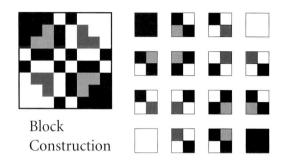

Block Construction

But wait! You have probably already noticed the hearts in this design. (I didn't see them until a friend pointed them out, but then I have occasionally been called heartless.)

Let's make the hearts a different color than the positive-negative colors (red being my favorite, I chose red.)

If we make the hearts the same color, and I think a reasonable contrast from either of the positive and negative colors, we can rotate alternating blocks 90° to enhance the weave. It kind of gives a flower effect as well.

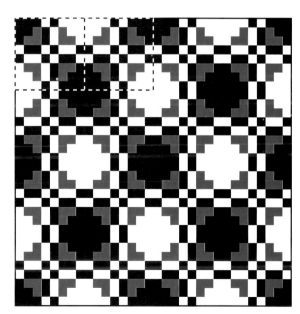

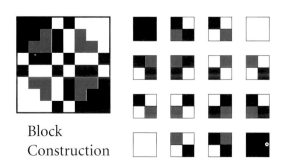

Block Construction

Now that we have sort of gotten a bit away from true positive and negative, let's stay away for a little bit and modify the first block.

The differences that can be achieved with a simple change in the block design can be astounding.

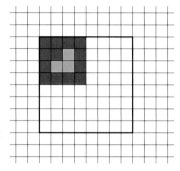

This time the four patch is all dark, except for the heart shape in the middle.

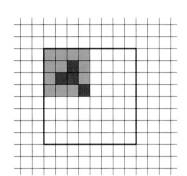

Again, repeat the four patch, completely opposite of the first one (light where dark was and vice versa.) But, this time add a dark square at the base of the dark heart.

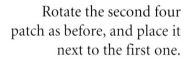

Rotate the second four patch as before, and place it next to the first one.

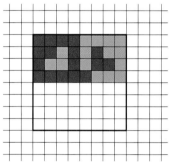

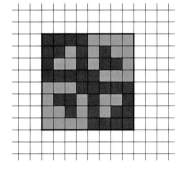

And, as before, duplicate these, rotate 180°, and place under the first two.

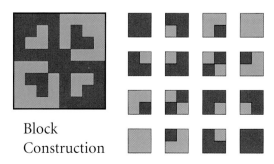

Block
Construction

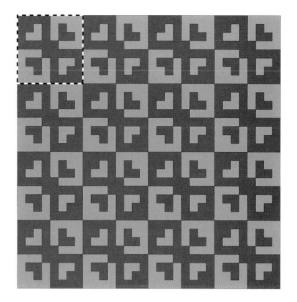

The design looks entirely different when the blocks are alternately rotated 90°. Hmmm. Perhaps if different colored triangles were added to the corners of the block to provide diamonds in the centers of the "squares"…

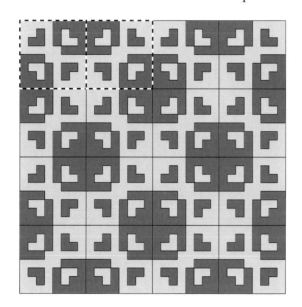

Here is the block in a kind of "barnraising" setting. It also might benefit from a few carefully placed triangle pieces in the block.

Theogene's Choice
41" x 49"

Fun With the Four Patch
54" x 54"
pieced and quilted by
Barbara Spielberg

An Evolutionary Idea

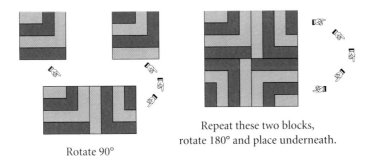

Rotate 90°

Repeat these two blocks,
rotate 180° and place underneath.

I started out with the idea of putting together a block that required a smaller amount of cutting and sewing, simply using two contrasting fabrics sewn together in strips. The idea was to not have the two patches pieced (simply cut from the strips.)

The constructed four patches look like the ones above left, and the positive-negative eight patch block is constructed in the same way as previously shown.

This design is its own negative when rotated 90°.

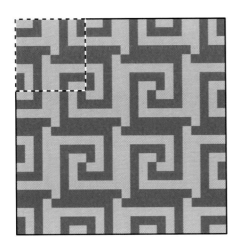

However, I thought there might be more to this. So, since the four patches were half and half contrasted colors, why not simply use one of the four patches and alternate it 90°? The result will not be a positive-negative design, however.

The result is rather different. Kind of a disjointed effect. Sort of like the way my mind works. I guess that's why I like it.

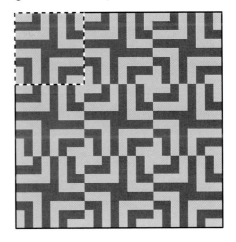

The next step is to look back at the first block and the way the blocks go together (the design is shown in black and white here.)

An important point (which you will see again later) is that a repeated block design (no block rotation) can be created using a variety of blocks. Any block defined by an eight patch square placed anywhere on the original design will work.

So, let's take the block defined by the dashed box (an eight patch square) inside the design. This block is created by merely swapping the four patches of the original block across the diagonal.

Now, to construct the design, rotate alternating blocks 90°. Something nice happens. We get the same figure in positive and negative intertwined. This effect is same as you have seen in Milky Way.

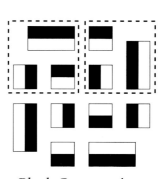

Block Construction
(two main four patches)

But wait! Is there anything we can do with this little figure that pops out of this design?

Note that the figure we have created here intertwines with itself. Therefore we might consider setting up blocks to allow multiple colors of this figure and do some other neat things. I'll let you do your own decomposition on this one.

The number of fabrics necessary to keep the figure distinct is five. I have included six in the design below. The background fabric (black here) is used in interior figures and white is added in the corners to weave into the background in the corners.

This is a tough one, since there are a large number of different blocks. The basic block construction is the same for the blocks, but the arrangement of fabrics is different in each. The layout to the right shows the different blocks involved. The starred blocks are the same block for the black fabric, but the other colors are different in each block.

6	8*	7*	7*	7*	7*	9*	6
9*	10*	11*	11*	11*	11*	10*	8*
7*	11*	1	2	3	4	11*	7*
7*	11*	3	4	5	1	11*	7*
7*	11*	5	1	2	3	11*	7*
7*	11*	2	3	4	5	11*	7*
8*	10*	11*	11*	11*	11*	10*	9*
6	9*	7*	7*	7*	7*	8*	6

This might be a good group project, since all blocks are made from the same sized strips (except perhaps for the outside rounds). The blocks could be divvied up among the members of a group.

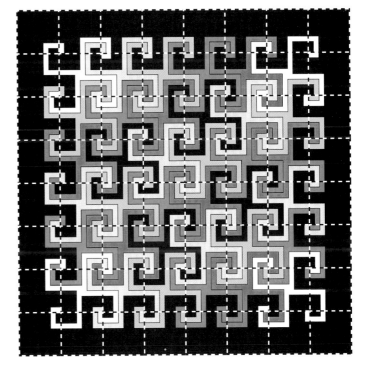

THE LAST STEP IN THIS EVOLUTION

Finally, let's take one last look at the last block (not that monster on the previous page) and do some manipulation of the sizes of the pieces.

The design is quite different with the wider arms on the figure and the squares in its center.

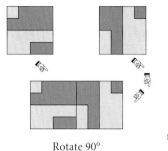

Rotate 90°

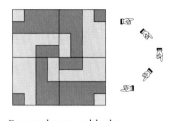

Repeat these two blocks, rotate 180° and place underneath

Block
Construction

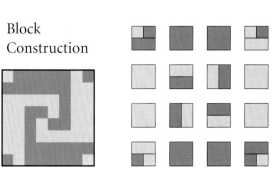

Egyptian Fantasy
45" x 54"
quilted by Leta Brazell

Not a Dear John Letter
64" x 85"
pieced and quilted by
Tula Bailey

Yin& Yang

In the process of positive and negative "Blocreations" it occurred to me (it sometimes takes a while for things to associate inside my brain) that the ultimate positive and negative was the ancient oriental Yin and Yang symbol. This should be my personal symbol, since it seems like I don't usually know whether I'm coming or going most of the time.

Apparently you can make a block out of this. It fits the mold of the 180° positive-negative association. To make it somewhat "rounded" you must cut corners (a must for me to get anything done.)

I tried this with the same block orientation for all blocks, and it gives a wavy look to the pattern. However, alternating every other block by 180° gives a more interesting appearance. Try some different layouts. This one is simple and can be fun.

Block A Construction

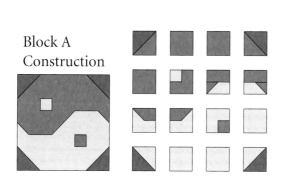

Block Layout

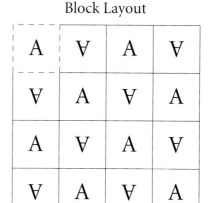

Yin & Yang
31" x 31"
pieced & quilted by
Edith Mitchell

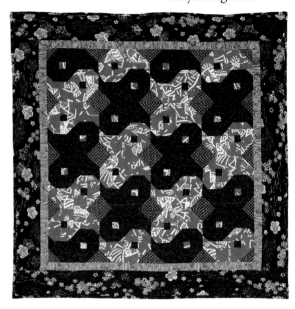

Yin & Yang
42" x 42"
pieced & quilted by
Kaye England

TSK TSK TSK
NO WONDER!
POOR WOMAN!

Dr. Ribbonkopf ponders the stuff that Mrs. Smith has been working on and sees the problem.

QUILTING PRIMER: STRIP PIECING

Mary is folding her fabric for cutting. She is folding it over a chair. No, no, Mary. You must fold it flat!

Mary is chagrined. Can you say chagrined? Can you say embarrassed? Are you chagrined? Are you embarrassed that you can't say chagrined?

Mary now reaches for her rotary cutter. Be careful, Mary! It is sharp. Oops! It is sharper than Mary. Mary has given herself a little cut. Get the band-aids, Mary. Mary must open a band-aid and put it on. No, Mary. Put it on the cut.

Mary now will cut strips. Cut, Mary, cut! Stop, Mary, stop! Oops! Too late. Mary has cut all of the fabric into strips. She realizes that she first must figure out how wide they should be. She also needs to make them straight. Bad strips! Bad, bad, bad. It is too bad that band-aids don't fix bad strips. Can you say %☆#@✳&? Mary can.

After a quick trip to her local quilt shop, Mary will now fold the fabric, measure the strips and cut what she needs plus a few extras to cover her mistakes. Mary cuts a lot of extra strips.

Now Mary will sew her strips together and then measure how much to cut off of the strips to make her blocks. Be careful Mary. Oops! Mary's blocks will look strange.

Mary must now make her blocks. Watch Mary string them through the machine. Sew, Mary! Sew! Oops! Mary's bobbin ran out of thread 20 blocks ago. Whoa, Mary! Whoa! Put the axe down. Oops! Mary now has a dented machine, not to mention a dull axe. Now Mary really has an axe to grind. Can you count to 20? *With* your shoes on?

LESSONS TO LEARN

1.   The important lesson is to PLAN AHEAD. Make sure you have everything you need for a project before you start. Once you have done this, you can be confident that you won't have to run out to get stuff more than a handful of times.

2.   When using a rotary cutter, you must use a cutting mat to protect the surface of your table. Mary forgot this as well, but the cuts in the table were masked by the axe marks where she missed the sewing machine.

3.   You must learn to count to 10 before you start, if for no other reason than to think before you strike. Also, you won't have to take off your shoes.

TO BE CONTINUED...

As you know, blocks are like tiles that you put together. Since they touch each other, you can make designs that are a continuation throughout the quilt, but are made up of only one block, or perhaps two blocks. An eight patch block provides lots of creativity room.

The left side of a block touches the right side of the next block (which may be a repeat of itself, which means it touches its own right side.) Similarly, the bottom touches the top of the block below, and the corners touch the opposite corners of the diagonal blocks.

This means that, unless the block is a simple design (e.g., a flower surrounded by background), there are design effects that you get simply by repeating the block. With this in mind, here are some blocks that concentrate on these relationships.

First, let's create one, step-by-step:

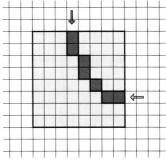

Draw in and connect some pieces that touch the sides of the proposed block.

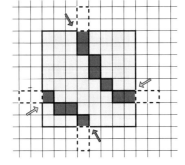

Draw in more pieces that touch the opposite sides in line with (or no more than one square above or below) the first pieces. The rule is that what goes out a side comes in the opposite side.

Draw pieces that touch a corner of the block. The continuation out a corner of the block is into the opposite corner.

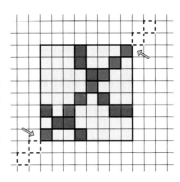

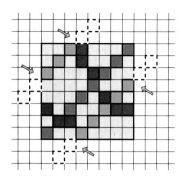

Now let's add another "strip" parallel to the red one. To do this start on the left side (it doesn't matter where, really) and add squares diagonally, remembering the rule.

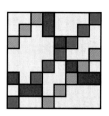

So, here we have a block that continues into itself.

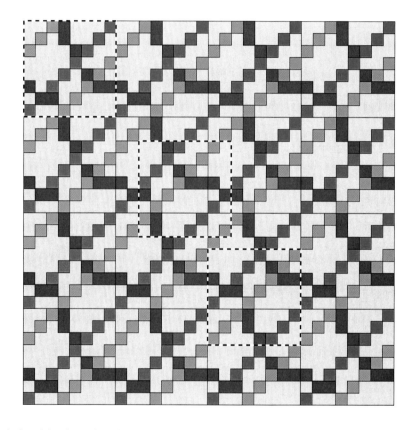

We have designed this block to be the repeat in the design. That is, the entire design of the pattern is contained in this single block.

Recall that there are many ways to put such a block together. Let's take the three blocks "carved" out of the 16-block design here. The first one is our original block. Note that a 16-block setting of the other two yields the same design.

Since you can put the block together in many ways, perhaps you'll find one way that is easier for you than another.

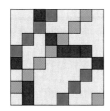

As you can see, the overall design stays the same regardless of the block starting point. So, sketch it out on paper and see if there is an "easiest" block to make.

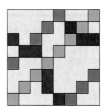

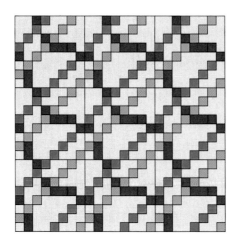

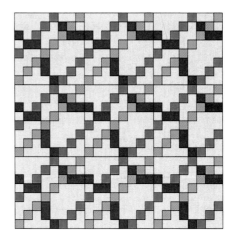

LET'S PUT THE RULES IN SOME SEMBLANCE OF ORDER:

1. When you move a piece out of a block to the right, it enters the adjacent block from the left.

2. By the same token, when you move a piece out of a block to the left, it enters the adjacent block from the right.

3. When you move a piece out of a block to the bottom, it enters the adjacent block from the top.

4. By the same token, when you move a piece out of a block to the top, it enters the adjacent block from the bottom.

5. Combining these steps, when you move a piece out of a block to the bottom right, it enters the diagonal block from the top left.

6. When you move a piece out of a block to the top right, it enters the diagonal block from the bottom left.

7. When you move a piece out of a block to the bottom left, it enters the diagonal block from the top right.

8. When you move a piece out of block to the top left, it enters the diagonal block from the bottom right.

NOTES ON 90° ROTATION AND CONNECTED DESIGNS

Block A

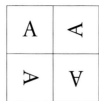

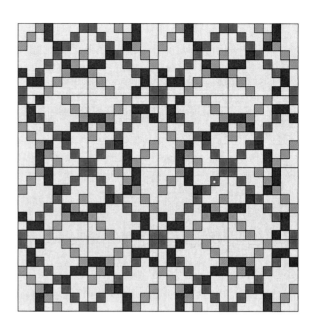

Let's apply some twisting and turning to the original block… in 90° increments. This gives us a four block repeat. Hmm. Could be interesting. Things are a little disjointed though.

The orange "strip" and the blue "curves" are the parts that appear disconnected. Let's see what happens when we change the block a little…

Three Squares

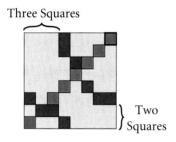

Two Squares

Two Squares

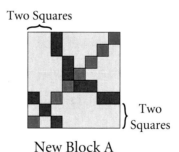

Two Squares

New Block A

Let's adjust the "curve" to line up as indicated above. Note that this block is symmetric across the diagonal (the red "strip") and lines up when it is rotated 90°.

Block A   Block B

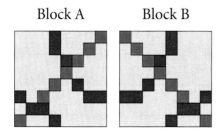

As you can see, when Block A is rotated 90°, the "curves" will not directly line up. One way to get this to happen is to put together two blocks – Block B a mirror image of Block A. The repeat is then four blocks

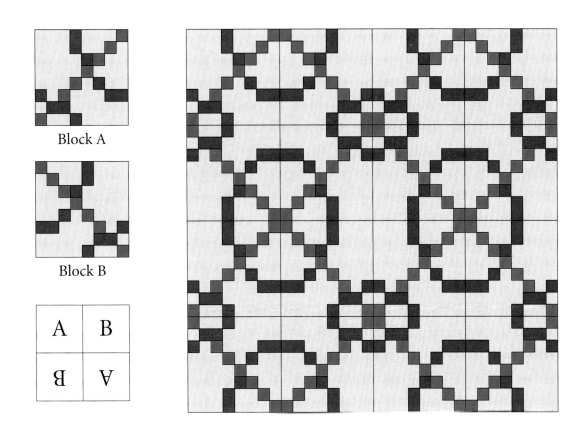

Block A

Block B

A	B
ᗺ	∀

Notice the shapes resulting from the "curves". Nonsymmetric mirror image blocks give ovals and the symmetric single block results in circles.

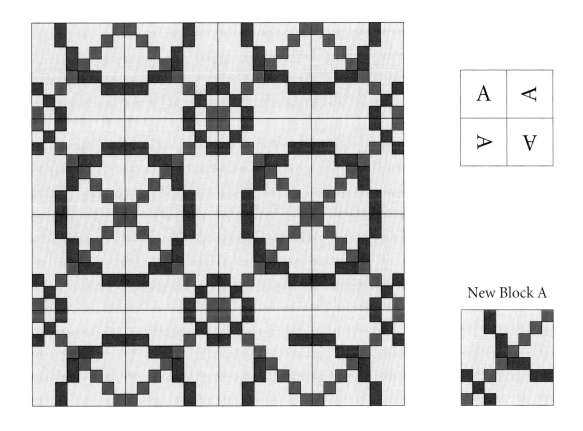

A	∀
∀	∀

New Block A

QUILTING PRIMER: SEWING MACHINES

A sewing machine is a machine that sews. It is a labor saving device. Can you say device? Do you have any devices? Do you have any vices? Can we talk?

How does a sewing machine save labor? Because it lets you sew faster. You can sew and sew and sew. Or, if you are slow like Mary, you can only sew.

Because you can sew more, the sewing machine lets you sew more fabric together before you see you have sewn the wrong sides together on 20 strips. How many four letter words can you list that are synonyms for "golly"?

The sewing machine lets you learn to unsew and unsew and unsew. Or, if you are slow like Mary, it is easier to cut new strips.

Mary likes labor saving devices. That's why Mary's sewing machine is at the flea market this weekend. (Can you say bargain? How much of a bargain will it be with all those dents?)

LESSONS TO LEARN

1. Sewing machines can be very useful to quilters to put things together. They can also be used to do actual quilting. However, as Mary has found out, your sewing machine can turn on you. So, it is important to turn on it first. (One way to turn on it is to not turn it on.)

2. Once you have sworn off your machine and tried the alternative, you will start to miss your machine and you will start to feel kindly towards it again. The subsequent lesson is that once your machine turns you on once again, you must turn it on. If you are like Mary, you must first go back to the flea market to see if it is back up for sale. You can't miss it. It's the one with the dents.

An Evolving Blocreation
(Really Playing With Blocks)

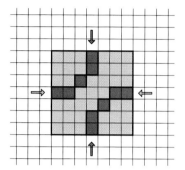

Let's take a look at an interesting block that has the features not only of symmetry across one diagonal, but across both, and can be lined up with itself in any orientation (the continuation is lined up in every direction.) Here we will have a single continuation at the center of the block. The block must be an n-patch with n being odd; ours will be a 7-patch to allow some variety and flexibility in design enhancements later.

The starting point here will be a curve from one side to an adjacent side. So, let's see what this gives us in overall design flexibility.

First, we'll simply line up the blocks with no twisting and turning.

Then we can rotate every other block 90°. Note that rotating 180° gives us the original orientation.

Then, let's try some irregular rotations.

Block A

A	A
A	A

Unrotated blocks provide a "curved" design that, to me, resembles chickenwire. This has some possibilities which I will explore later.

Rotating every other block 90° gives the circles we saw earlier, except that here they are equal in size.

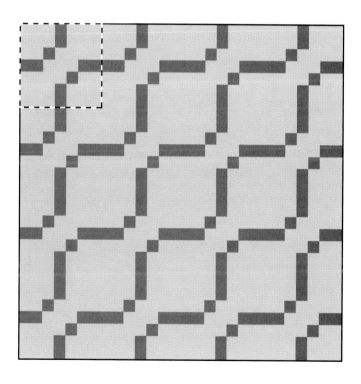

GET IT TOGETHER!

Here I want to randomize the layout a little bit. First, I took two blocks (both Block A), unrotated, and put them next to each other. Then I placed two Block A's rotated 90°, underneath the first two. Then I repeated this four block set (B) with every other four block set rotated 90°.

Next, I took these 16 block sets (C) and put them together with every 16 block set rotated 90° to form a 90° symmetrical 64 block set (D).

There are a multitude of ways to put these kinds of blocks together.

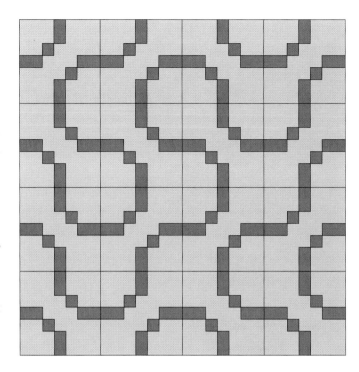

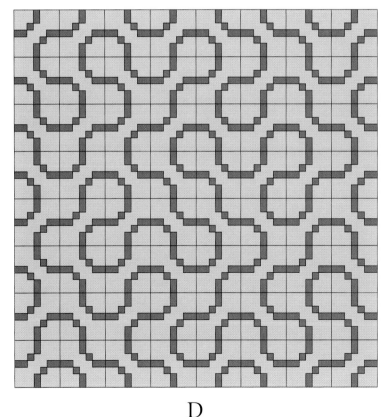

D

Block A   Block A'

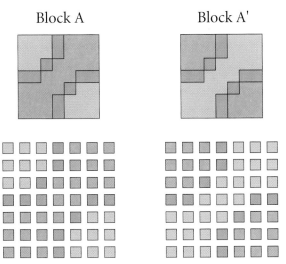

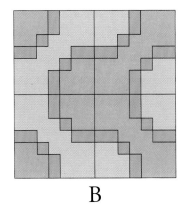

B

Note that the seven patch blocks are split out into the individual patches to show construction. Your approach to construction is up to you.

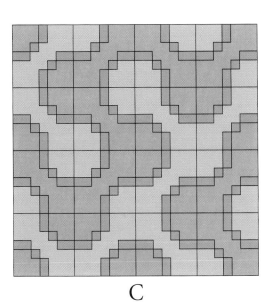

C

The maze effect of this pattern suggests that we investigate two colors of background. So, what if we make the background in the corners of the block "negatives" and then make a "negative" of the block (Blocks A and A'.)

Then, put these two together in much the same way as we did with the single block. An interesting effect arises. Try ocean and land fabric themes.

D

ONE STEP BACKWARD AND TWO STEPS FORWARD

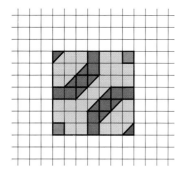

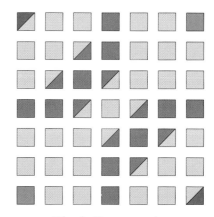

Block Construction

Going back to the original seven patch block, let's add some triangle pieces to smooth out the "curves" and add a little variety.

Let's also add triangles and squares in opposite corners to see the effect.

Rotate every other block 90° to get a four block set and put these sets together with no further rotation to get the final design.

Block A

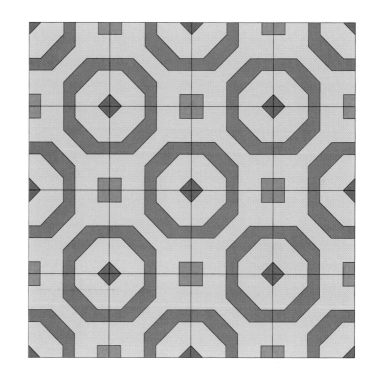

Block Layout

This adds a little something to the design, but what if…

Shadows in the Quilt

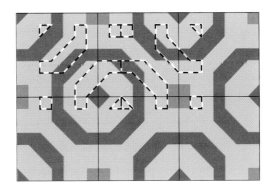

There are essentially two blocks to which the shadow will be applied.

Let's apply a shadow to all of the non-background pieces in the blocks for the previous design. This means that, since every other block is rotated 90°, there are essentially two blocks. This is because the shadow must be in the same relative position in each block. We can't start with a block and put in a shadow and then rotate every other one.

For this design, let's shift the shadow over two squares and down one.

On paper, I draw the outlines of the pieces in the two blocks and shifted by the appropriate amount (here indicated by the dashed lines.)

Notice how the shadow pieces overlap other blocks. We will use the rules (slightly adapted) to determine where these pieces go in the two blocks.

The figure to the right labels the overlap pieces 1-8 and indicates how they become pieces in the two blocks (labelled 1a-8a.)

The rules are shown in the shaded box on the next page.

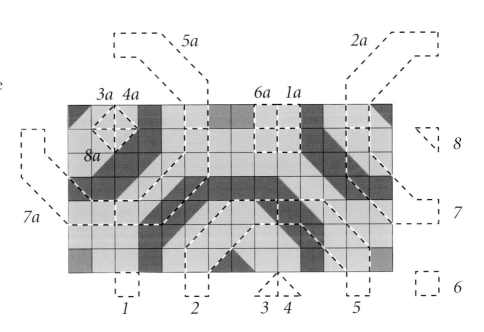

ADAPTED RULES

When two blocks are repeated alternately and a shadow is applied, the references to continuing out the sides, bottom, top, or diagonals now mean that they continue into the alternate block.

The fabric for the shadow pieces should be a darker value of the same color family as the background (the same pattern, if available.)

An important note: once you have shifted the pieces and aligned them for the shadow, the shadow will not appear where the original pieces in the blocks are – the shadow is in effect underneath.

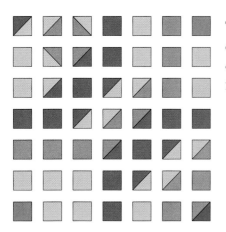

The two blocks are a little more complicated because of the shadows added. However, the layout for the quilt is the same as for the circles. The repeat is a set of four of these blocks (two each, alternated.)

Block A

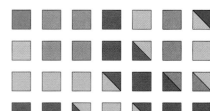

Shadow Blocks
Block Construction

Block B

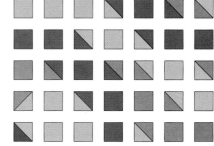

A	B	A	B
B	A	B	A
A	B	A	B
B	A	B	A

Block Layout

Walter Goes for the Gold
51" x 65"
pieced and quilted by
Edith Mitchell

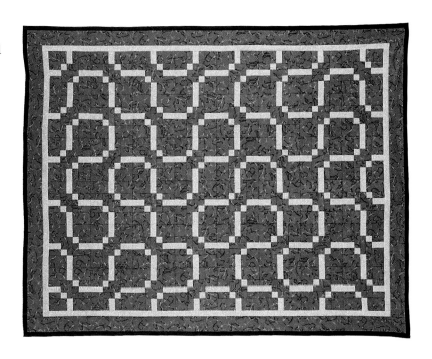

Dr. Ribbonkopf after the patients have gone.

Quilting Primer: Quilt Guilds

Now Mary is really into quilting. She must now seek out people with similar interests since her spouse and family have lost interest. Can you say crony?

Mary will go to a guild. What is a guild?

A guild is a group of people who all do the same thing: they all belong to the same Guild.

A *quilting* guild is a group of people who meet and talk about quilting. They learn all about politics and committees and the need to frequently elect officers. Can you say "lame duck"?

Mary will learn to volunteer to serve on committees. Soon Mary will learn to keep her hand down and her mouth shut.

Guilds have meetings. Meetings are fun and Mary can talk with friends about friends. Mary will attend the meetings religiously to protect her reputation. Sometimes at these meetings, guild business is conducted.

Guilds make money for guild functions and stuff by charging for functions and selling stuff. Can you say "stuff"? Can you sell stuff? Gee, Mary, doesn't that dented sewing machine over there in the corner look familiar?

Lessons to Learn

1. The quilting guild is a veritable hotbed of activity. You can learn new techniques, new designs, and other new information about friends who don't show up at the meetings. But that's not all! You will be able to do "challenge" quilting – kind of like bullfighting with designer capes, but without the bull. (Weeelllll, maybe *some* bull.)

2. It is important to be accepted and be with people you like and people who like you. But the guild meetings will probably do for now.

MY RULES OF THUMB ON FABRIC REQUIREMENTS

Break the basic block into its elementary square (i.e., the 1-patch.) This is probably the basic square you will have used to design your block.

1. Determine what you want the finished block size (assuming a square block) to be. Divide the block size by the number of squares in a block width.

2. Add two seam allowances to the finished square width (e.g., if ¼" is the seam allowance then add ½".) This is the elementary square unfinished width.

3. Determine the number of blocks in the quilt.

4. Count the number of squares covered by each fabric in the block. (Include the whole square if a square has a 45° triangle of that fabric in it.)

5. Multiply the number of squares per fabric by the number of blocks.

6. Multiply this number for each fabric by the elementary square unfinished width.

7. Divide by 45 (assuming a fabric width of 45") to get an approximate number of strips. Round this up to the next highest number and add a couple of strips to allow for error.

8. Multiply the number of strips by the elementary square unfinished width. Round this up to the next quarter yard.

This is a fair estimate of the amount of fabric needed for your quilt. Any extra can be added to your scrap boxes (if strips and/or pieces are already cut) or to your stash.

An Example

Take the seven patch block (before the shadows are applied):

1. Since this is a seven patch, let's make it easy on ourselves and say the *finished* block size is 7". Therefore, the *finished* square size is 1".

2. Assuming a ¼" seam allowance, the unfinished square size is 1½".

3.   Assume we want a 5 by 7 block quilt (35 blocks total.)

4.   The block breakdown gives us:

Squares with red fabric:	2
Squares with gold fabric:	37
Squares with brown fabric:	18
Squares with light blue fabric:	2
Total:	59

(number of squares + 10 extra for squares with triangles)

5.   The number of squares per fabric is the number of blocks times the number of squares per block:

Squares with red fabric:	2	x	35	=	70
Squares with gold fabric:	37	x	35	=	1295
Squares with brown fabric:	18	x	35	=	630
Squares with light blue fabric:	2	x	35	=	70

6.   The "length" of each fabric is the respective number of squares times the square width:

Squares with red fabric:	70	x	1½" =	105"
Squares with gold fabric:	1295	x	1½" =	1942½"
Squares with brown fabric:	630	x	1½" =	945"
Squares with light blue fabric:	70	x	1½" =	105"

7.   The number of strips of each fabric is the respective "length" divided by the fabric width (assuming a 45" wide fabric here):

Squares with red fabric:	105"	÷	45"	=	2⅓	(make it 3)
Squares with gold fabric:	1942½"	÷	45"	=	43⅙	(make it 45)
Squares with brown fabric:	945"	÷	45"	=	21	(make it 23)
Squares with light blue fabric:	105"	÷	45"	=	2⅓	(make it 3)

8.   Finally, the number of yards of each fabric is the respective number of strips times the width of each strip (the unfinished square width) divided by 36 inches per yard (numbers in parentheses are conservative numbers *I* might use to cover *my* mistakes – for me, even this might not do it):

Red fabric:	3	x	1½"	=	4½"	÷	36"	=	⅛	(⅜)
Gold fabric:	45	x	1½"	=	67½"	÷	36"	=	1⅞	(2⅛)
Brown fabric:	23	x	1½"	=	34½"	÷	36"	=	.96	(1¼)
Light blue fabric:	3	x	1½"	=	4½"	÷	36"	=	⅛	(⅜)

Ribbons in the Quilt

IMPRESSIONS OF RIBBONS

In playing with tilings of lines going through the design, I first concentrated on two fabric designs. However, I started to insert multiple color families. From this playing came a series of designs that looked like ribbons to me. Thus the name.

The designs here were created with stripped piecing in mind. The first designs use only squares and rectangles. Shortly you will see similar designs with triangle pieces to provide more definition to the ribbons.

This first design uses a lot of background fabric. The choice of fabrics for all of these designs should include four strong color families (although you might try only two) and a contrasting background, which may be lighter or darker. There are two basic 4-patches in each of the two blocks. Construction of this one will be quick and easy.

Block A   Block B

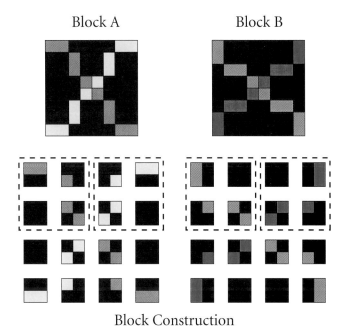

Block Construction

Block Layout

A	B	A	B
B	A	B	A
A	B	A	B
B	A	B	A

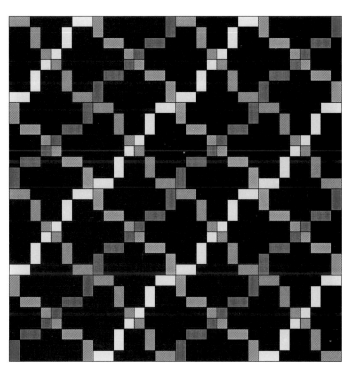

Amish Ribbons
37" x 37"

JuJuBees
46" x 46"

ENTWINED RIBBONS

Here is a little twist on the Ribbons theme. Take the four colors and make a half twist starting at the top center (or left center) of the block and bowing out to the side and back in to the bottom center (or right center) of the block. Do this for each color. To get the effect of continued twisting, alternate rotating the blocks 180°. The block can be constructed with paired strips (color fabrics together and colored fabrics with background fabric.) See the construction shown to the right.

Different patterns develop with different placement of the basic block. Try some.

Block A
Construction

Block Layout

A	∀	A	∀
∀	A	∀	A
A	∀	A	∀
∀	A	∀	A

A	A	A	A
A	A	A	A
A	A	A	A
A	A	A	A

A	A	A	A
∀	∀	∀	∀
A	A	A	A
∀	∀	∀	∀

Try one of these layouts

Block A

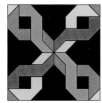

Block A

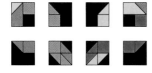

Block B

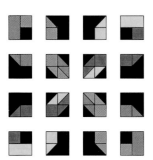

Block Construction

BRAIDED RIBBONS

We can take the first Ribbon design and combine the two blocks with a little twisting and turning and change to simulate ribbon entwining. With the addition of some triangle pieces to simulate rounded corners, we have a design that is a little less impressionistic than the others.

The second block is the same as the first with the exception of corner pieces from two of the fabrics to give the cross-over effect at alternate corners.

Try this design with this single block.

The repeat consists of the straight placement of the two blocks alternately.

A	B	A	B
B	A	B	A
A	B	A	B
B	A	B	A

Block Layout

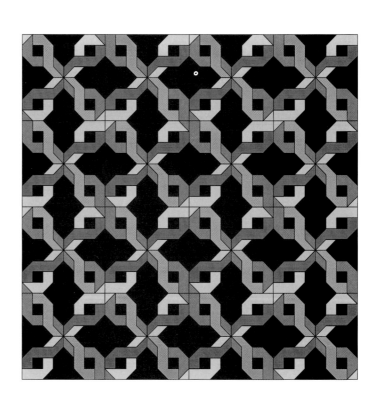

STRANDS WITHIN STRANDS

And now for another complex block. This one is the result of working with the "Strands" and playing a little "what if …" game on a piece of paper. I wanted the tiled effect, so I made sure that the strands continued from one block into the next. It started out as a four fabric pattern (three strand fabrics – two intertwined and one separate – and the background.) I decided to use the twists in the strands to give a little dimensionality to it. This meant adding three more fabrics (darker values for each strand) to give a shadowed effect.

Block A

Block Layout

A	A	A	A
A	A	A	A
A	A	A	A
A	A	A	A

Block Construction

Quilting Primer: Quilt Market

Sadie is a shop owner. Sadie must go to market.

At market, she will buy stuff to sell at her shop. She will buy fabric and patterns and thread. (Oh my!)

Sadie sees lots of stuff. Buy some stuff, Sadie! Buy, Sadie! Buy!

Look at Sadie knuckle under to the salespeople. Can you say knuckle? Can you say under? Can you knuckle under like Sadie?

See Sadie's pen fly. Soon Sadie will run out of checks.

See Sadie's eyes when she remembers she can order C.O.D. Can you spell C.O.D.?

Soon Sadie has gotten all she needs and some she doesn't. Sadie must now get it all home. See? C.O.D. isn't so bad sometimes.

Sadie is pleased with her purchases. It has been a good market for Sadie. She will go home and sell her purchases to her customers in her shop.

It is time to bid market adieu until next time. Sadie is melancholy at the close of market. Can you say sad? (Melancholy is probably out of the question.) And because Sadie hates to say goodbye, she slips away without being seen.

See a satisfied Sadie sadly sag as she surreptitiously schlepps into the sunset. Can you say that three times really fast?

Lessons to Learn

1. A quilt market is an exhilarating experience for Sadie. The crowds! The color! The camaraderie! The friends! And once she gets on the airplane to go to quilt market the flight is sometimes fun, too. When she is finally at the market she looks, she shops, she orders! Fabric, patterns, (this book,) and a multitude of other things to sell to her customers back home.

2. If Sadie didn't do this, her quilt shop might be dull. That is, if she didn't have customers like Mary, who keeps Sadie on her toes. Actually Mary is a ballet teacher and swaps steps for stash. This is one reason Sadie is so agile at quilt market.

Chickenwire

Now, let's take that one seven patch continuation block that I said resembles chickenwire (well, it does!) and extend it to an eight patch (easier to make.) The chickenwire effect still exists in this design, but it is not quite as "symmetric".

Remember, we have to ensure that the design pieces at the edge of the eight patch will line up with the opposite side when the blocks are placed side-by-side.

The rest of the designs in this section are based on this simple block with some additions, and once in a while, some rotation. I think they can be a lot of fun, especially on those days when you're "cooped" up and need some kind of activity to wile away the time.

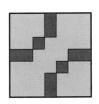

Original "Chickenwire"

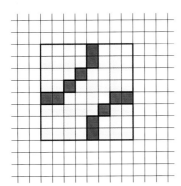

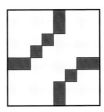

Extra Crispy

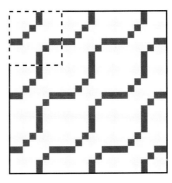

The fun now begins as we add some stuff to this block. For starters, let's add a shadow to the main design, the main design here being red. The fabric for the shadow should be a darker shade of the background.

The shadow effect is based on a shifting of the main design pieces to the right one square and down two squares. Now the "chickenwire" effect is more apparent.

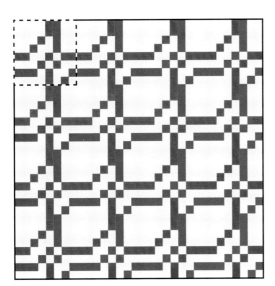

Spicy

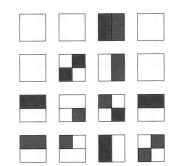

Block Construction

Block A

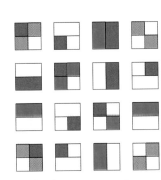

Block Construction

Basic Layout

Now we add a little center piece inside the chickenwire. To do this, simply add some alternate color pieces at the corners of the block and include darker background pieces for the shadow effect. Not a bad look with the block in the same orientation. However, when we rotate blocks around in 90° increments, something happens and we get what I dubbed the "F" quilt. (My usual grade.)

Basic Repeat

ADDING LINES AND ABSTRACTING SHADOWS

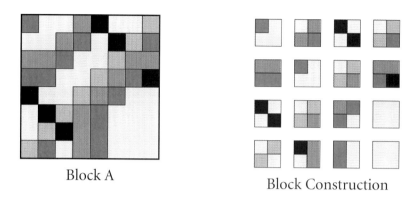

Block A

Block Construction

Let's take the previous block and add some lines and things to it. Here the shadows have been drawn up to the "chickenwire" and slightly abstracted. They aren't true shadows any more. However, they give the shadow appearance. Adding lines on the opposite diagonal and making them a totally different color gives a more varied look. Lines in the same direction reduce the "chickenwire" effect and give it a little different look. Making these diagonals a slightly different color, gives a blended appearance.

Now this design lends itself to some more playing. Just look at those open spaces…

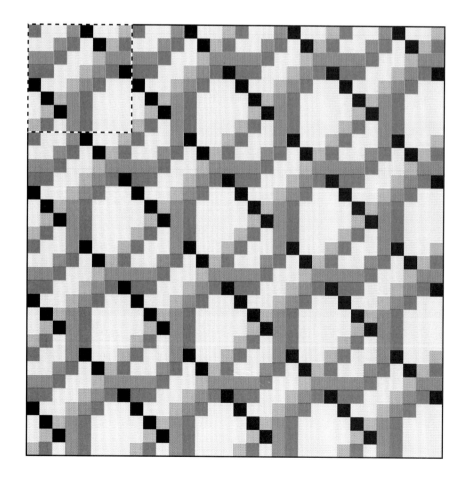

A	A
A	A

Basic Layout

FILLING IN THE BASKET – FLOWERS AND HEARTS

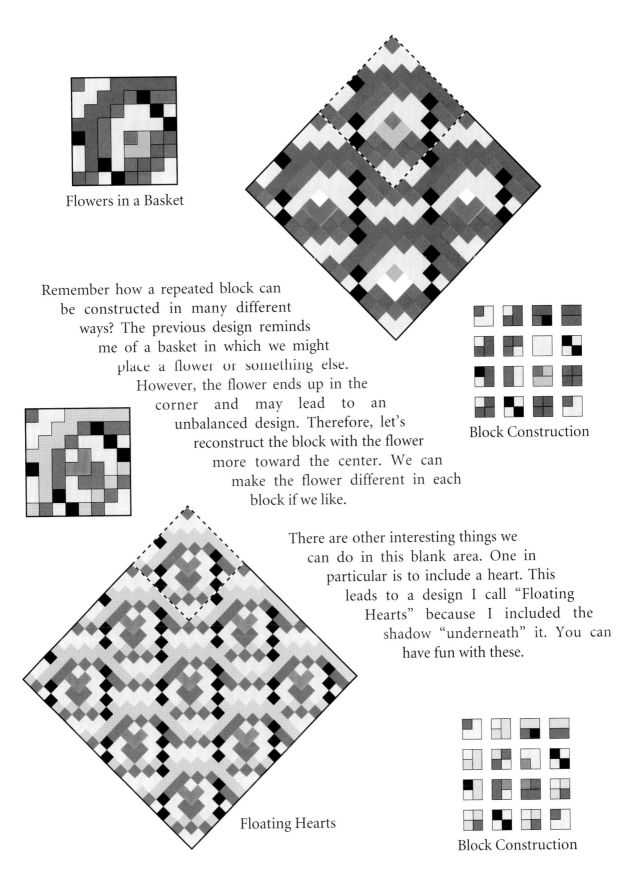

Flowers in a Basket

Block Construction

Remember how a repeated block can be constructed in many different ways? The previous design reminds me of a basket in which we might place a flower or something else. However, the flower ends up in the corner and may lead to an unbalanced design. Therefore, let's reconstruct the block with the flower more toward the center. We can make the flower different in each block if we like.

There are other interesting things we can do in this blank area. One in particular is to include a heart. This leads to a design I call "Floating Hearts" because I included the shadow "underneath" it. You can have fun with these.

Floating Hearts

Block Construction

THE THREE FABRIC SPECIAL

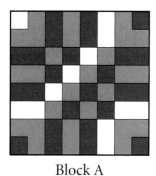

Block A

Block
Construction
Alternatives

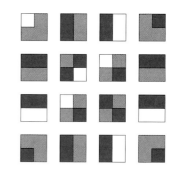

Here we take advantage of our knowledge of the continuation rules and put in two "strands" of a darker fabric and one "strand" of a lighter value of the same color family, all on a very light background. (Your color combination is up to you.) To make it interesting (since the corners come together in a "circle") I put in a center with a missing piece to give the impression of depth.

Again, since this is an unrotated, single block, the block can be constructed in many ways.

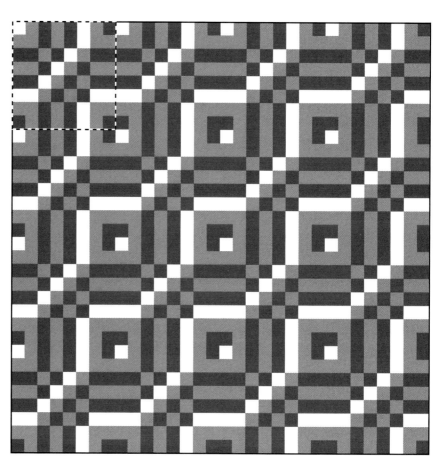

A	A
A	A

Basic Layout

MOUNTAIN VALLEY FOG

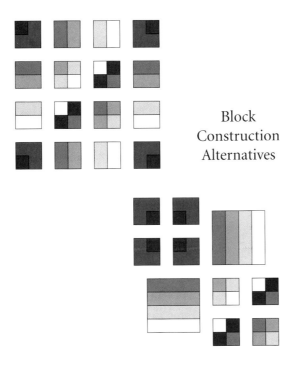

Block
Construction
Alternatives

Block A

Finally, let's take the continuation to the extreme and make the entire quilt design continuation pieces. Here I have proposed that the design consist of six fabrics, all of the same color family. These will blend into each other to create the design.

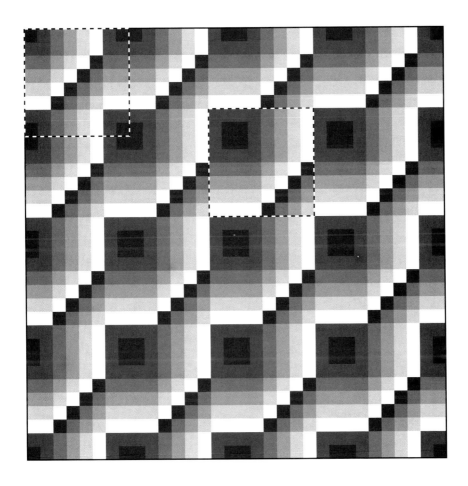

This is basically the same design as the previous one, but the background has now been replaced with the other three fabrics.

This one gives sort of a kaleidescopic effect. Try it on the diagonal. The impression I get is of mountains with fog in the valleys.

A	A
A	A

Basic Layout

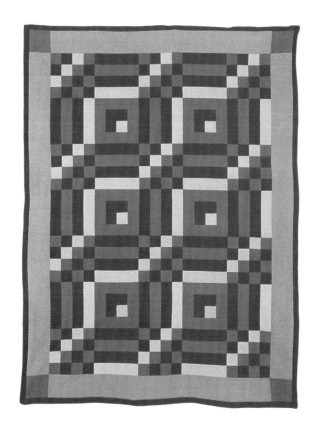

Red Licorice
38" x 50"
pieced and quilted by
Jean Humenansky

J-Team Blues
42" x 42"
pieced and quilted by
Jenny McDermid

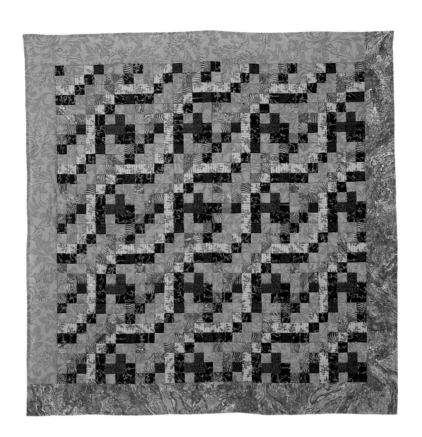

Floating Hearts
46" x 46"
pieced and quilted by
Jan Krueger

Dr. Ribbonkopf's secret desire to be
a chicken received a serious setback
when Mrs. Smith described the
"chickenwire" designs.

TRIANGULATION

The Simple
Two Patch

Now, we look at a very simple block that has powerful capabilities when combined with your expertise and imagination. This is a simple two patch that can be made from two strips and connector corners. This little block can be put together in so many ways, it boggles the mind. Perhaps your mind is not boggled as easily as mine. (Actually, the operation of a toaster boggles my mind.)

I have tried a few designs here that use all of the techniques I have talked about in earlier sections, except for shadows. This block yields beautiful positive-negative designs (since it is its own negative when rotated 180°.)

Let us see what ensues.

Start by rotating every other two patch by 180° to get a four patch.

Now put four of them together, rotating in 90° increments. This yields a 90° symmetric eight patch with a florette design.

Putting these eight patches together, you definitely see that the design is completely positive-negative.

Another Simple Two Patch
(Mirror Image of First One)

This design starts with the mirror image of the two patch on the previous page. The positive-negative on the previous page appears to be meshed so that there is a distinction between the two contrasting fabrics. When we do the design on this page, there is an overlap of the positive-negative structure.

The basic block

Note the alternate block is the negative of the block I used. Also, you see the positive-negative "circles" that make up the pattern with overlapping tiles.

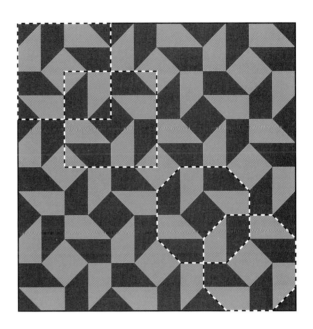

Another interesting thing to do is to look at the layout without any color and see what little designs "pop" out at you. For example I see the figure I have outlined. This has some interesting possibilities and will probably be worth exploring. If I only had more time...

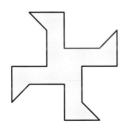

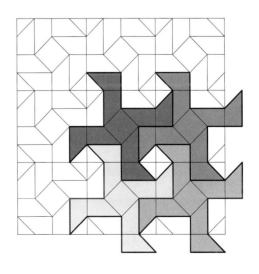

The Original
Simple Two Patch

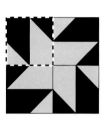

Take the two patch from the first page of this section and put four together, rotating in 90° increments.

Now, put these together and we have a neat little positive-negative star pattern.

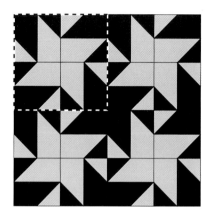

What happens, however when we rotate the two patches in 90° increments in the opposite direction?

This gives us the star we saw on the previous page. Now, let's look at this in the "plain" view and see what "pops" out…

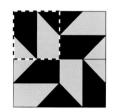

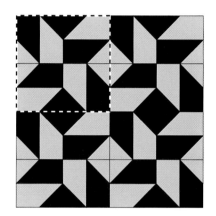

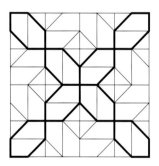

The "plain" view looks different for this mirror image block. What I see is the "ribbony" effect that I have highlighted. The design below is based on this effect and, with the two values in the two color groups, gives a lattice look.

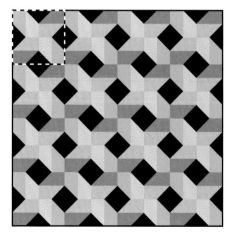

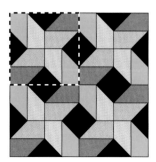

The two, two patches for this design.

(Not to be confused with repairs to ballet costumes.)

BBQ
58" x 58"
quilted by
Susan Godkin

The Wedding Quilt
78" 112"
quilted by
Leta Brazell

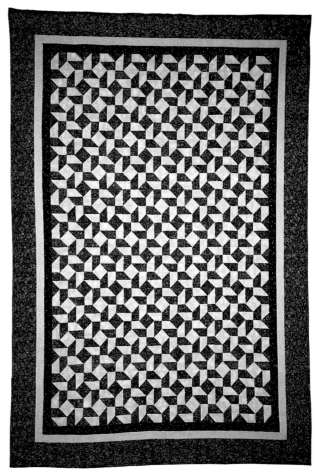

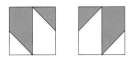

The Mirror Image
Two Patches

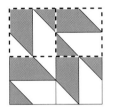

Take the two mirror image two patches from before and put them together by rotating one 90° and then alternating them.

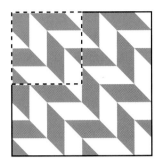

Now, put four of these four patches together to make an eight patch. Notice the braided effect this gives.

Finally, put four of these together, rotating in 90° increments to make a starburst design.

BRAIDED STARBURST

Let's take this braided effect to an extreme. Keeping in mind the starburst effect, what if we let each "braid" in the above eight patch be a different color, but all in the same color family? (Make sure to keep the same background in all blocks in the design.)

Such a block is shown below in blues. If we make the starburst design and repeat it, we get a pretty good blended lattice design. There are seven different two patches involved in making this design.

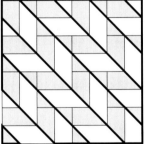

Note the Braided Effect

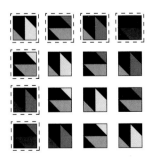

Block Construction

BLOCKS WITH LOTSA TRIANGLES

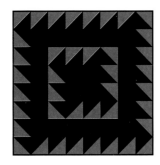

Let's look at a couple of blocks that anyone who likes to make triangles will really get a workout on. This first one (which I call "Cutting Edge") was designed to be 90° symmetric – any rotation yields the same block.

Although this block requires a myriad of triangles, it is relatively easy to make. It only requires construction of two, two patches.

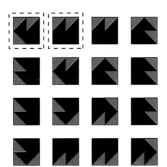

Block Construction

There are a lot of ways to use fabrics and a lot of design enhancements that you can use for this one. A couple of block changes are suggested below. I think the variation in background fabric has potential (see the layout below.)

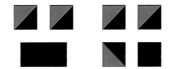

There are two main
two patches in this block.

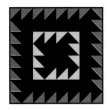

Alternative Blocks

If we add some additional triangles to the previous block we get the first block to the right. This by itself is interesting, but I propose adding a mirror image of the block and alternating it in the quilt layout.

This design (seen below) has been dubbed "Circling Geese" because of the geese made when the mirror image blocks meet. Each block is an eight patch and has three basic two patches in its construction.

Notice the way the background around the geese forms an interwoven effect…

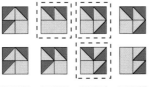 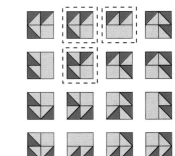
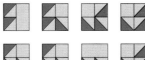

Block Construction

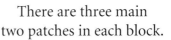

There are three main two patches in each block.

Suppose we use different colors to make the background next to the triangles on the outside of the eight patches? On the left and right sides of the eight patches we should use a different color than that for the top and bottom. The effect when these are put together is interesting.

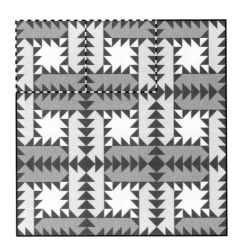

HELLO, ACME RESTRAINTS?
UH...HOLD ON A MOMENT.

MRS. SMITH! NO! PUT THE
TRIANGLE QUILT DOWN! IT HAS
SHARP CORNERS!

Sawtooth
45" x 45"
quilted by
Leta Brazell

Circling Geese
57" x 57"

Obviously, Dr. Ribbonkopf needs to find a therapeutic outlet.
Any suggestions? To Be Continued...............